Happy Ending?

AF528974

OrangeBooks Publication

1st Floor, Rajhans Arcade, Mall Road, Kohka, Bhilai, Chhattisgarh 490020

Website: **www.orangebooks.in**

© Copyright, 2025, Author

All rights reserved. No part of this book may be reproduced, stored in a retrieval system, or transmitted, in any form by any means, electronic, mechanical, magnetic, optical, chemical, manual, photocopying, recording or otherwise, without the prior written consent of its writer.

First Edition, 2025

ISBN: 978-93-6554-173-1

Price: Rs. 235.00

The opinions/ contents expressed in this book are solely of the author and do not represent the opinions/ standings/ thoughts of Orange Books.

Printed in India

Happy Ending?

Aabha Soni

Orange Books Publication
www.orangebooks.in

Contents

"He smiled- and only she knew why?

Loves crazy feeling, and for once, neither

Felt deprived."

1

Teenage Dream

He's a poetry

I wish I didn't want to end with a goodbye.

Because we deserve a perfect life,

Where   am his girl and he's mine.

Because we look so beautiful every time,

Like destiny is in favour of me first time.

We are compatible,

For a love story which lasts for long time.

He and I are very alike,

His eyes say every time.

When I talk nonsense,

He still smiles.

Why is he so nice?

Am I falling in love with this guy??

His name flashes in my mind,

Every time I listen to a romantic song.

Or writing a poem about my happy times,

He sometimes gives me reason to survive,

And moreover, every day happy time.

I didn't meet him a long time ago,

Still, he knows about me and my favourite crime.

Things are going so well this time,

Do you also believe this is God's sign??

He's healing all my scars,

Even though he was never the reason for those ones

When he's around,

Time passes so fast.

Where days feel like a few hours.

I can't believe we were strangers once.

What a dream, I must say

Don't wake me up, dear,

Even if it gets very late.

We are so in the moment

It scares me some days.

What if he also disappears within a few days?

2

Oh, My Dear Stranger

We started as strangers,
Now heading together.
Your hands fit mine so perfectly,
As they're meant by destiny.

Accepting me for who I am,
Loving me for who I am.
Putting together to make me happy,
You are genuinely my best journey.

You look beautiful when you smile,
When you blush every time.
When you look in my eyes,
It says we are meant for a long time.

I admire our bond,
Will always be thankful to God.
For sending you in my life,
loved by the most beautiful guy.

Moreover, you're such a beautiful soul.
I never felt like this for anyone before,
You’re the person I was waiting for,
Even when I lost all the hopes.

Even after all of my all flaws,
You always make me feel strong.
Giving me best days of my life,
I will always admire you for my whole life.

I hope this never ends,
As you're most incredible thing to this mess.
You make everything so much perfect,
Thank you for being my best man.

3

On My Mind

You're my morning thought,

And evening smile.

Well, why are you,

Staying in mind every time??

You're just a person,

I didn't meet a long ago time

Why is everything changing in my life?

I want to listen only to this guy,

because , he's giving me little butterflies.

I am seeing my future in his eyes,

Just beautiful and bright.

Like his smile.

He’s my reason to get,

Overwhelmed sometimes.

Because he's the one who really keeps Alive,

A kid inside me resides.

You're my little boy.

Am I really in love this time?

Will he ever let me??

Call him mine.

Because I am a mess,

And he’s perfect for me every time

He feels like home,

He’s healing all my wounds.

Since we met first time

What is this happening to me?

When I want promised not to fall for another guy,

I don't want him to be.

One more lesson of my life,

I am hoping for a good ending this time.

4

You Are My Home

You're eyes lead,

Me to write.

You're smile makes,

me feel all the butterflies.

You're a guy,

I was waiting for a long time.

With you all, my emotions are alive,

I don't feel numb like old times.

Your reasons for making me smile.

I am still wondering,

What did I do to deserve?

You are in my life.

You will be my favourite topic.

When I write,

Because I felt,

Love with you at first sight.

Your warmth feels,

Different every time.

It shows trust,

That you hold for me every time.

Every day is good around you,

Home feels just with you.

Time passes so fast,

Hours pass like a couple of minutes. of ours.

Views with you are always beautiful,

As you consider my scars.

Maybe this is a happy ending,

Where we will be each other's halves.

5

Casual Him?

His height is fine, not 6 Feet
Just looks cute with my little height.
His smile is my favourite part
As it's wide and bright.

His one call bring Happiness to my face
He says I am his lady and please stay.
His random urge to say, I love you
Always enlightens my day.

His jealousy is so real
When I take someone else's name.
As I am his wife
And we are bound by vows of life and sake.

His anger toward me

When I don’t make time for him, it's so insane.

When I don’t give him attention

Like he gives me every day.

I know he’s in love with me

Even he didn’t say that.

Those words in a filmy way

There will be a happy ending,

Of us in so many ways.

We will still be 60

His eyes will be my favourite.

And his smile will keep my day enlightened.

His face will be the first thing,

And his smell will be my happy place.

he will be my ending

I believed to was happy in so many ways

He’s not just a casual stranger

I am going to forget as the days pass by.

6

Power Couple?

People say we look good together.
And I like such things when I hear,
But in the while my heart shivers.
Because I know there is no future,
Everything is very clear.

People say we can see love in your eyes.
And I somehow believe they are right,
Coz you are the one.
Who can fill all my empty voids,
Just within seconds.of time

People say you are gone crazy.
I guess why wouldn't I?
Coz I found my lover, soulmate,
And a partner in crime.
Why wouldn't I??

People say you will leave me someday.
Somehow, my mind already knew,
This is from the very first day.
But still ending up choosing you every day,
Coz that's what we do in love's sake?

People say you deserve better.
But I am looking for nothing,
Just you in every other person.
I failed every time.

People say time will heal.
But what can? I do,
Coz time doesn't change anything,
I still love you.

People say we are destined together.
But I don't believe in that any further,
Coz directions and path are very unclear.
Like you never believe us to be here.

"If the whole world is watching, I will still choose you, over and over again, just to be with you."

7

Do Eyes Lie?

I can't forget those beautiful eyes,

I remember that little spark in there.

When I used to call him mine,

He acted fine.

How I am not supposed to fall,

For him, every time?

Where his eyes say he is mine.

Because I still can't forget his beautiful smile,

When I used to give him.

All my precious time,

He was acting really fine.

I wish I could do anything,

To stay with him for a while.

Now I can't forget any of that time,
He was really good at pretending all the time.
Why he's done acting this time,
Doesn't he miss me like old times???
I want to stay with him for the rest of my life.

Because everything felt real at that time.
He was the perfect man to be mine,
I want to know.
Why did he do all of these at that time?
When did he love me back any of time?

Because now I can't move on from him,
He is the love of my life.
Like I was his for that time,
Eyes can’t be a lie?
Says my heart every time.

8

Things I Never Wanted

I never wanted to be the villain of your story,
There wouldn't be anything such as ending.
I wanted to be there as glory,
With lifetime story.

I never wanted to be the reason for cracks in your heart,
Or our reasons to be apart.
I wanted to heal your scramble heart,
From all the past guards.

I never wanted promises to be made,
Or say things that I never meant to say.
I wanted to be your person,
With whom you don't think before you say.

I never wanted to be the reason for your crumbling soul,
Or the reason that you don't believe in anyone anymore.
I wanted you to stay,
And listened to me for one another day.

I never wanted you to walk away,
By saying, forget all those days.
I want you to stay,
And walk a mile with me for a day.

9

Love Is Curse

He said,

He loves her,

Like flowers

But end up

Plugging her into the graveyard.

He said,

He loves her like sunset,

Where she was the sun

And he was waiting for her to set.

He said,

He loves her like a bird,

But ends her up in the cage

To show her rage.

He said,

He loves her like a tree,

Where she wanted to give him a shadow.

But he ends up burning her.

He said,

He loves her like a rainbow,

Where she wanted to be.

Loved in grey and white.

Ironically,

She loves him

Like moon

No matter how incomplete or complete

Always beautiful.

10

Destiny Plan

Destiny, didn’t want your ring,
To fit well in my hand.
I don't curse you,
All the things that we ever had.

At the end of the day,
I was never love of your life.
Although you used to say that every time,
From our first kiss,
To goodbye.
How far we have come in our lives.

Where we recognise,
Each other as strangers.
With deepest darkest secrets,
Of each other’s.

Why destiny preordained,
To me like this every time.
How can I curse you?
For the things I always liked.
When all you give me a good time?

It was tough for me,
Maybe you were not ready to love me
I was in love with you at this time.
But it was my fault, right?

You were just trying to be nice,
Helping me out in my tough times
I still mention you,
In front of every boy
Coz you were the one for me,
I believe made for me this life.

11

Veins of memory

It was the hardest goodbye, I must say

I wasn't there before,

When I was forced to cut my veins.

Where I was struggling to breathe every day

My soul completely shattered in every way

When someone used to say your name.

All I blamed was me

For giving you a piece of my heart

But you hurt me anyway.

I gave you power

To tear my universe in every way.

You were the one who healed me

In some ways.

Still, you were the reason for much deeper cuts anyway.

Let me take you back to the very old days
Where you were the medicine to my pain
Relief for all my losses halfway.
Scars you cured within some days.

Now, Scars are getting deeper every day
Will I be able to heal them anyway
I am cursed for not being loved
As anyone's favourite girl
Every time, all I get are much deeper cuts.

12

Himand My Mind

When she smiles,

He's in her head.

When she tries to breathe,

His perfume fragrance was all over her head.

When she zones out,

His summer stories in her head.

When she is excited about something,

His happy place is in her head.

When she's sleepy,

His forever dreams must be in her head.

When she’s quiet,

His voice must be echoing in her head.

When she's being clumsy,

His queen treatment in her head.

When she's battering,

His smile is all in her head.

When she's blushing,

His one glimpse in her head.

When she holds, your hand,

His Touch is in her head.

When she's looking at the sky,

His promises of watching stars together in her head.

When someone asks her out,

His thoughts never leave her head.

"Start was beautiful dream, end is nightmare indeed."

13

Illusion Of Us

Beginning and ending,

It both lasted long.

With the hope of not hanging up the call.

Happiness and tears of joy on the first call,

Asking for closure

This time, when you are gone.

Numb eyes and a fake smile.

When you took away from me,

One of the main reasons for me to survive.

Awkward silence still part of this game,

On the first call, it was shyness.

Moving on converted to silence,

Walking around with you on the street.
And now alone screaming nights in grief.
Was I hard to believe?

Slowly accepting the fact you're gone
Begging didn’t last much
Time feels like moving on

One day we will meet again
Like strangers with no pain.
Where we are just soulmates.

14

Forgotten Promises?

Your hands are around her waist,

Your happiness is on face.

Your efforts are reflecting,

Where you said “I mean everything”

Are you capable of loving her?

Coz, you said I am your last love.

Where we imagined our future.

With lots of kids and my fav pups.

Your words again echoing in my mind,

While you might be sleeping with her in meanwhile.

Telling her your fav bedtimes,

That’s my destiny

Where I gave everything.

Once that was my place,
Your arms were safest for me, I must say.
I remember myself whispering,
And saying I want to be like this every day.

You never mentioned to me,
About this lady's love?
Coz I was you’re dream girl.
Did you even consider before sleeping with her?

Love in your eyes for her,
I am not sure where you are?
Took seconds of time to shatter my heart,
To see her so close to your arms.

Coz, you said I am the only person,
To get that place as your half.
Are you messing up with her?
But then why are you bringing her flowers?

16

Unfinished Goodbye?

It was so soon,

For you to go yet.

You promised me for so many years,

Where we will stick to each other.

I miss him so bad,

Why are you always on my head?

Every night I remember his face,

Before going to bed.

People are just not good for me yet,

I am damaged, destroyed and deteriorated left.

No one is meant for me yet.

Because you were everything I ever loved to get.

Goodbye is unfinished for us,

Soulmates aren’t always lovers?

Life is a long journey

Where love this time felt like misery.

16

Journey Of Hii and Bye

He's my favourite Hii,

And the hardest goodbye.

Things with him just passed by,

Within seconds on time.

Was he ever mine?

He used to told me I'm his,

Lovely baby pie.

But took seconds of time,

To turn around and say goodbye.

He was holding me from my waist,

Where I was so lost.

Got in the moment phase,

I was about to kiss himin those days,

Which turned out into good- bye haze.

I wish he had stayed.
I was asking him for some time to,
Show him all the love,
I have been holding on for so many days.
Where he didn't have faith.

I was so excited to meet him,
Got his favourite flower.
And his favourite music taste,
I was ready to be his girl,
But he said it's too late.

Crying in the mid night,
Trapped in his memories.
I lost myself again,
In the process of
Hi and bye, I must say.

17
His New Girl

Where are you?

Hiding in a pathway.

Or hiding in her arms?

Which you said

You don't like anyway.

Why are there tears in my eyes?

When you are still residing nearby.

Are you with that lady?

Making her smile.

But you said I don't need to mind.

What about you're plans

Of staying as my man

What's your plan?

To stay with her

because now she's your lady, I guess.

Why am I up at 3?
Just looking out for you on the street
Where are you?
Making promises with her,
One of my darkest fears indeed.

What are you looking for?
Loving her from your deep heart?
Or playing smart
Because once I was a victim
Of your cards.

Why it is so hard?
Coz I still dream about you even when we are apart
What are you dreaming about?
Her as you're another half?

Why can't you stay real, as you're
You're a good human,
Once believed in my heart.
Do you really want her?
Coz, I remember our start.

What am I supposed to do?

When I can't unlove you.

Will she be able to admire you?

Or she's gonna leave you

Coz karma sometimes hits too.

18

Fairytale Ends

I never thought,

We will be strangers again.

I always knew forever existed in fairytales,

But our story wasn't less than a fairytale.

The person who used to make me laugh,

Who helped me move on?

Who gave me the real meaning of love?

Why are you ignoring me now?

The person who always gave me a shoulder,

To cry on let me brag about my life

When it was a piece of shit

Why are you now lying?

The way he used to look at me

With that crappy beautiful smile

When distances meant nothing

Being with each other was everything

Why isn't he with me this time?

When I’m fighting with my own mind

Where my heart says he's not a bad guy

Where my heart believes he's still by your side

He was firstly friend of mine

Why can't we just be with each other tonight?

We will talk to each other

Will try to make things right.

Coz, I believe in a beautiful ending.

Not a fairy tale but a real story.

Why can't we just forget everything?

Acts like nothing

We were never normal

I was a messy problem

No one ever loved me the way you did

Then why you have to pretend you don't give a shit?

My doors are always open for you.

Coz I never found a lover like you.

Time is playing a game with us

But we will find ways to overcome this up.

"Just like sunflowers, I will glow again, I am not your rose anymore. but I will find my sun and will to love again."

19

Wonder

I wonder if you miss me

I miss you every day.

I wonder do you still walk

While on the phone call?

I wonder why I don't smile anymore

Even when the clock strikes 7 nowadays?

I wonder do you still separate

Time to talk about your day?

I wonder you would still feel jealous

Of the time lost without spending with u?

I wonder do you still believe in good

Or you just believe being at your own?

I wonder do you call her babypie?

Like I was on our days.

I wonder do you still talk about

Me in front of your friends?

I wonder what if our paths cross again one day

Will u smile at me like the old way?

I wonder if one day

Will you ask me to come back or give me a start back?

20

Distance Or Time?

Time is slipping away,
You're just getting far away.
Your home is no longer,
Few steps away.
In spite it turning out to be miles away

Time is slipping away,
You're just getting along with the day,
Roaming around with some friends and bay,
No longer makes time for me in a day.

Time is slipping away,
We never realised.
How much have we grown from,
From ranting about days.
To take a little less every day,

Time is slipping away,

Destiny made its own way.

From separating our paths,

To unite them for some day.

Time is slipping away,

And I'm trying to move on every day.

Yet ends up daily,

Remembering that pretty face.

Time slipped away,

Makes me miss you every day.

Now I remember you,

Just by a glimpse of those days.

21

Hate That I Still Love You

You say I should hate you,

What can I do?

When I feel my soul is bound

With you.

Every time I try to hurt you,

My heart bleeds.

Every time someone curses you,

I can't breathe.

Every time you say,

You can't live.

Part of my heart,

Skips a beat.

Every time you get tired,

My body.

Start aching,

Like it desires you're heat.

Every time you feel sad,

My little child,

Unable to handle that.

In a good deed.

You curse you're self,

For the things you did to me.

But my heart knows,

That I have forgiven you from my core deep.

Still, you say I shouldn't,

Take care of yourself like

It's me.

What am I supposed to do when

My heart is cursed for me.

It feels everything that u feel,

It’s a feeling that never leaves.

I can’t hurt you,

When it hurts me.

22

Human Diary

You were hope for me on my bad days,
Made me feel happiest on my best days.
Talking to you used to make my day,
You called me, you're happy kiddo, back in those days.

Where things went, I can't rant.
I look for you in every other guy,
I still feel you when romantic songs,
Or the letter I write.

When I go on long drives,
I always crave your hand on my thighs.
Life is so lifeless, these days even when I am alive.
Coz my mind craves for you every time.

When any romantic song strikes,

My main hero will be you as old times.

It's a Lovely feeling to feel you,

Even when you left me so soon, back in time.

This life is a nightmare,

When I can't see your shoulder, I want to cry.

You were always one call away,

To make me stop crying.

It's abaca, I am not lying,

Every day I open my eyes, it feels cursed
Why am I alive?

I got some friends,

But they don't understand like you
used to do it every time.

I remember me being a kid,

Where you appreciated all my shit.

You left me so vulnerable,

My words can't define.

I want to complain you about this,

Coz you were my dairy for life.

23

From Stranger to Stranger

He said hi,

She blissfully replied.

He said I like your voice

Calls her every day and night.

To check whether she's fine.

Stalking her every night,

Sending her a voice note

About the love of life

Thinking about her every night

Time passed very quickly by

She was neutral all the time

Coz he was just a random guy?

Spending day and night together
Now, he knows her well
From her favourite song to her deepest secrets
They don't feel like strangers now?

He gets mad when she asks him to leave
Or whenever she resits to eat
Or whenever she sees other guys
Like, she is his favourite crime?

Time was passing by
They are no longer talking like
She's No One to Him
He doesn't remember her favourite food or memories
She decided to keep him forever in her mind
Coz he was more than a random guy?

She still remembers his likes and dislikes

Every time he passes by

Her heart aches

Coz he's not just a random stranger

She used to call him mine.

Time passed by

From strangers to friends to lovers to haters
to strangers again.

Who knows the deepest secrets of each other's?

24

My Last Seven Minutes

He will be my seven minutes after life,

My soul will remember him,

Even after I am done with this life.

His memories will make me feel alive again.

He will be my seven minutes,

His smile will be my favourite.

His voice will always echo in my mind.

Coz he is the one who made me believe in
Love at first sight

My mind will be full of his memories,

It will remember all those 3 words and promises.

The way he held me,

The way he used to scold me.

All the promises he made.

It will be my last seven minutes,

To remember all good days.

I will pray to God,

Although my mind is full of his thoughts.

Still just want to get a glimpse of ours,

Until my brain wouldn't stop.

Where had you held my hand

How you kissed me on the head

How you looked at me when I was mad

To keep us forever

Because I was everything you ever wanna have?

The pain when you were leaving our home town.

And promises not to forget,

Until we meet like, Time has stopped.

Oh, my seven minutes, I am scared,

Will you be enough? To remember
everything like I want.

I will be counting my last breaths

Yet he'll be one in my mindset.

It will take 7 minutes again

To make me relive all those days

Although I will die soon

But it will be a peaceful death.

"In the end, it never ends."